NASCAR Champions

RYAN NEWMAN

Nicole Pristash

New York

Published in 2009 by The Rosen Publishing Group, Inc.
29 East 21st Street, New York, NY 10010

First Edition

Book Design: Michael J. Flynn
Layout Design: Kate Laczynski
Photo Researcher: Jessica Gerweck

Photo Credits: All images © Getty Images.

Library of Congress Cataloging-in-Publication Data

Pristash, Nicole.
  Ryan Newman / Nicole Pristash.
      p. cm. — (NASCAR champions)
  Includes index.
  ISBN 978-1-4042-4450-4 (library binding) ISBN 978-1-4042-4546-4 (pbk)
  ISBN 978-1-4042-4564-8 (6-pack)
  1. Newman, Ryan, 1977– —Juvenile literature. 2. Automobile racing drivers—United States—Biography—Juvenile literature. I. Title.
  GV1032.N44P75 2009
  796.72092—dc22
  [B]
                                    2007049965

Manufactured in the United States of America

Contents

Ryan Newman races cars for NASCAR. He is called Rocketman because he became a good driver so quickly.

4

Ryan started racing when he was four years old. He **admired** NASCAR drivers.

In 1993, Ryan began racing small race cars called **midgets**. This helped him become a better driver.

8

Ryan soon began racing big cars. He moved right up to NASCAR's top **series** of races.

In 2002, Ryan had a great year. He won his first Winston Cup race and the **Rookie** of the Year **award**.

Part of Ryan's racing team is called a pit **crew**. The pit crew works on Ryan's car during a race.

14

Ryan also drives in NASCAR's Busch Series. In 2005, he made history by winning five races in a row!

Ryan likes to spend time with his wife, Krissie. Together they help raise money for animals that are in danger.

18

19

In 2007, Ryan finished five races in the top five. He hopes to keep getting better and to win a Sprint Cup **championship**.

20

Glossary

admired (ed-MYRD) Looked up to.

award (uh-WORD) A special honor given to someone.

championship (CHAM-pee-un-ship) A race held to determine the best, or the winner.

crew (KROO) A team of people who work together on a job.

midgets (MIH-jets) Very small things.

rookie (RU-kee) A new player or driver.

series (SIR-eez) A group of races.

Books and Web Sites

Books

Kelley, K.C. *NASCAR Authorized Handbook*. Pleasantville, NY: Reader's Digest, 2005.

Riley, Gail Blasser. *NASCAR Technology*. Blazers, 2008.

Web Sites

Due to the changing nature of Internet links, the Rosen Publishing Group, Inc., has developed an online list of Web sites related to the subject of this book. This site is updated regularly. Please use this link to access the list: www.powerkidslinks.com/nascar/newman/

23

Index